Confirmation for teens

Lesson One

By Debbie Repp

Life has often been compared to a journey, an adventure toward wholeness and happiness, toward peace and fulfillment. Many of our most difficult moments are those in which we must decide which "path" to take. Especially during our adolescent years, the road that leads us to *genuine* happiness and inner peace is often very difficult to see.

Our society suggests a variety of appealing options. Movies, magazines, the media, and sometimes even our parents and educators make the "economic pathway to happiness" look like a sure thing. On this road, a high-paying job, financial security, and *lots* of material possessions become very important.

The "pathway of power and fame" appears even more glamorous — how often our heroes are outstanding athletes or beautiful movie stars. (And aren't these people *always* happy?) The world in which we live lures us toward these roads — and toward many more with grand appearances. We are bombarded with messages that tell us that wealth, fame, power, and physical attractiveness are all directly linked to contentment in one's life.

For the true Christian, however, there is more. Much more. The mature Christian knows that money, power, and fame have little—if anything—to do with genuine happiness. These things, in fact, too often leave us empty and aching.

The mature Christian knows that life is indeed a journey—*a journey of faith!* It is a journey that lasts a lifetime. The Christian looks to Jesus for direction and strength. He or she looks to Jesus when attempting to discover "the right path."

But how do we begin to know Jesus? How do we begin to allow him to show us the way? How do we make *him* our food for this great journey?

Encounters With Christ Through Our Church.

The Catholic Church offers help in our quest to know and be strengthened by Jesus. First, it offers a *community of believers*. We will not be alone in our Christian lives. Others will be with us. These others—the people of God—will be a major source of strength as we journey.

Jesus said, "For where two or three are gathered in my name, I am there among them" (Matthew 18:20). In the gathering of the community, the presence of Christ is found. Without the community, we could not follow the road Jesus calls us to travel. His word comes to us through this community. We become sons and daughters of God and heirs to heaven through baptism into this community. We are nourished in this community with the Eucharist, the body of Christ broken and shared by these people.

Jesus said, "For where two or three are gathered in my name, I am there among them."
MATTHEW 18:20

The Kobal Collection: Jesus Christ Superstar, Universal Studios

The Catholic Church also offers us the *sacramental life* as a way to encounter Christ. Traditionally, a sacrament has been defined as "an outward sign, instituted by Christ, to give grace." Put more simply, a sacrament is a special moment in our Catholic life in which outward signs and rituals bring us into a very intense closeness to Jesus. Through human ministries, Jesus is actually forgiving us, nourishing us, healing us. We are, in these very personal encounters with Christ, receiving his power so that we can follow in his footsteps.

Confirmation for teens

LESSON TWO

The Parish Commitment Ceremony

By Debbie Repp

As you prepare to receive the gifts of the Holy Spirit in the sacrament of confirmation, you will become involved in a period of important study, prayer, reflection, and service. It is most valuable if your parish family is fully aware of your work so that it can support you through prayer.

In **Lesson One**, we discussed how the Catholic Church offers us a community of believers so that we are never alone as we journey toward Christian maturity. Jesus tells us, "For where two or three are gathered in my name, I am there among them" (Matthew 18:20). In the gathering of the community, the very real *presence of Christ* is found. Without the community, it would become most difficult, if not impossible, to follow Christ. His word comes to us through this community. We became sons and daughters of God and heirs to heaven through baptism into this community. We are nourished in this community with the Eucharist, the body of Christ broken and shared by these people.

In confirmation, too, the community is essential. It is the faith community in which you worship that calls you to become stronger members. And *you* have much to give to the community! Your church needs the deeper faith, courage, and energy that new members can bring. In return, it responds to your desire for confirmation through its welcoming and its prayers. Though you are young, you are fully recognized as *people of faith* entering a very important time of preparation and discernment. Therefore, your parish family offers you its reassurance and support.

The prayer service which follows will ideally occur following the homily during a Sunday eucharistic celebration. The "Parish Commitment Ceremony" gives you the opportunity to promise to do your best to *understand* the sacrament of confirmation. (It is *not* your commitment to receive the sacrament — that comes much later!)

The ceremony also informs the parish family of your intentions so that all its members can be spiritually present with you as you journey.

Note: Parishes vary widely on when they ask confirmation candidates to select their "sponsors." If you have chosen a sponsor, ask him or her to be present with you at the "Parish Commitment Ceremony," but your sponsor's presence is not essential at this time. If no sponsors are present at the ceremony, omit the section of the ceremony entitled "To the Confirmation Sponsors."

This short service can fit into a paraliturgy or the eucharistic liturgy. It should be preceded by a reading from Scripture and followed by prayers for God's blessings on this preparation for the sacrament of confirmation. A homily by the priest or deacon or an encouragement from the catechist would also be appropriate before the "commitment to prepare." The celebrant names, one at a time, the candidates for confirmation. As the names are called, each will stand with his or her sponsor. The Words of Commitment follow.

In the gathering of the community, the very real presence of Christ is found.

Confirmation for teens

LESSON THREE

THE SACRAMENTS OF INITIATION

Our Introduction to the Life of the Church

In the Catholic tradition, baptism, confirmation, and Eucharist are known as the sacraments of initiation. Initiation is defined as "the actions, ceremonies, etc. observed in admitting a candidate into a society or organization." It includes "instruction in the first principles" of the society or organization. Through these "initiation rituals," new members experience a definite acceptance into the society and are expected to participate more fully in the activities and life of the society.

By Debbie Repp

Baptism, confirmation, and Eucharist — as sacraments of initiation — are our introduction to the life of the Catholic Church. Even though in our present experience these three sacraments take place over a long period of time, initially, they were celebrated *at one time.* After a long period of instruction centered on the beliefs of the Creed, the candidates (called catechumens) presented themselves to the Christian community for acceptance.

In the way that new members of the Catholic faith are presently welcomed into the Church on Holy Saturday night, candidates were baptized. On that same evening, the candidates were confirmed, signifying their personal faith commitment to be active members of their new Christian community. Then, for the first time, the new Christians were able to participate in the entire eucharistic liturgy and receive holy Communion. Since all three sacraments — baptism, confirmation, and Eucharist — were given at one time to new members of the Church, they were known as the sacraments of initiation.

This is still the order in which new adult Catholics receive the sacraments on Holy Saturday night. In a later lesson, we will discuss how these three sacraments came to be separated. There remains much discussion and debate within the Church as to when and at what age it is most appropriate to receive the sacrament of confirmation. Most catechists (those who instruct us in the beliefs of our faith), however, continue to regard confirmation as a "sacrament of initiation."

We Are Claimed for Christ by Our Baptism

When we were younger, perhaps even shortly after our birth, our parents started the "initiation process" for us by asking God's Church to baptize us. We were brought into the faith of the Church. The priest or deacon said to our parents: "You have asked to have your child baptized. In doing so, you have accepted the responsibility of training your child in the faith. It will be your duty to bring your child up to keep God's commandments as Christ taught you, by loving God and your neighbor." The ceremony continued with even more dramatic emphasis on the Christian community welcoming us into its life. "My dear child, the Christian community welcomes you with great joy. In its name, I claim you for Christ, our Savior, by the sign of this cross."

Baptism not only focused on our beginning journey into the faith of the community but also strongly stressed that we were loved by God and became God's very own. The Father of Jesus Christ became our Father, too. We are unconditionally accepted and loved by God. As we learned in **Lesson One**, our baptism gives us great *intrinsic value.* If for no other reason, we must see ourselves as precious and worthy of love simply *because we are children of the Lord.*

In Confirmation, Empowered by the Spirit, We Make the Faith Our Own

Baptism brings a person into the faith of the Church. As a small baby or child, we are completely passive, but the grace of God is freely given to us. Confirmation, as it is now celebrated, is largely the "active" part of the initiation process. The baptized Christian takes the faith that was given and makes

Confirmation for teens

LESSON FOUR

Compliant With *The Roman Missal*, Third Edition

We believe...

In the previous lessons, you learned that confirmation is one of the sacraments of initiation. Usually, before choosing to become fully initiated into a group or organization, it is wise to have a firm understanding of the beliefs, goals, and purposes of the group or organization. As a simple example, if you have an interest in becoming a writer for your high school website, you would likely study the website to see if it contains articles you would enjoy researching and writing. You might also find out when editorial meetings take place, what kind of time commitment a staff writer needs to make, and so on. Once you have a good understanding of the website's function and requirements, you will be able to make a well-informed decision about whether or not to join the staff of writers.

By Debbie Repp

With the help of the Holy Spirit, confirmation involves your commitment to become *fully immersed in the life of the Church*. Remember, confirmation is the *active* part of the initiation process. Therefore, preparation for confirmation requires careful and thoughtful study of the teachings of the Catholic Church. The better you understand the Church and its teachings, the more mature your decision to become an active and committed member.

In this lesson, we will review some of the most important beliefs of the Catholic community as revealed in our belief statements (the Nicene Creed and the Apostles' Creed) and in guidelines set forth by sacred Scripture (the Ten Commandments and the Beatitudes). Study these teachings carefully. Make sure you understand the meaning of each statement. Do not hesitate to ask for clarification if something does not make sense to you. When you ask questions, you open the door to greater understanding and growth.

The NICENE CREED

In the year 325, the Church leaders met in the town of Nicaea to consider what the Church held as sacred doctrine. This Council, drawing upon three hundred years of lived faith, formulated a creed that we still say every Sunday at Mass. Containing 14 different belief statements, it summarized many of the most important teachings of the community.

I believe in one God,
the Father almighty,
maker of heaven and earth,
of all things visible and invisible.

I believe in one Lord Jesus Christ,
the Only Begotten Son of God,
born of the Father before all ages.

God from God, Light from Light,
true God from true God,
begotten, not made,
consubstantial with the Father;
through him all things were made.
For us men and for our salvation
he came down from heaven,
and by the Holy Spirit
was incarnate of the Virgin Mary, and became man.
For our sake he was crucified under Pontius Pilate,
he suffered death and was buried,
and rose again on the third day
in accordance with the Scriptures.
He ascended into heaven
and is seated at the right hand of the Father.
He will come again in glory
to judge the living and the dead
and his kingdom will have no end.

I believe in the Holy Spirit,
the Lord, the giver of life,
who proceeds from the Father and the Son,
who with the Father and the Son
is adored and glorified,
who has spoken through the prophets.

I believe in one, holy, catholic and apostolic Church.
I confess one Baptism
for the forgiveness of sins
and I look forward to the resurrection of the dead
and the life of the world to come. Amen.

The APOSTLES' CREED

The Apostles' Creed, the first prayer of the rosary, is another belief statement of the Church.

I believe in God, the Father almighty,
Creator of heaven and earth,

and in Jesus Christ, his only Son, our Lord,
who was conceived by the Holy Spirit,
born of the Virgin Mary,
suffered under Pontius Pilate,
was crucified, died and was buried;
he descended into hell;
On the third day he rose again from the dead;

he ascended into heaven,
and is seated at the right hand
of God the Father almighty;
from there he will come to judge
the living and the dead.

I believe in the Holy Spirit,
the holy catholic Church,
the communion of saints,
the forgiveness of sins,
the resurrection of the body,
and life everlasting. Amen.

The TEN COMMANDMENTS

Besides the two creedal statements, which are the basic doctrinal statements of the Catholic community, two scripturally based guidelines have been standards for the moral life of Christians. The first of these Scripture passages is found in Exodus 20:1–17:

One *I am the Lord your God, who brought you out of the land of Egypt, out of the house of slavery; you shall have no other gods before me. You shall not make for yourself an idol, whether in the form of anything that is in heaven above, or that is on the earth beneath, or that is in the waters under the earth. You shall not bow down to them or worship them; for I the Lord your God am a jealous God, punishing children for the iniquity of parents, to the third and the fourth generation of those who reject me, but showing steadfast love to the thousandth generation of those who love me and keep my commandments.*

Two *You shall not make wrongful use of the name of the Lord your God, for the Lord will not acquit anyone who misuses his name.*

Three *Remember the sabbath day, and keep it holy. Six days you shall labor and do all your work. But the seventh day is a sabbath to the Lord your God; you shall not do any work — you, your son or your daughter, your male or female slave, your livestock, or the alien resident in your towns. For in six days the Lord made heaven and earth, the sea, and all that is in them, but rested the seventh day; therefore the Lord blessed the sabbath day and consecrated it.*

Four *Honor your father and your mother, so that your days may be long in the land that the Lord your God is giving you.*

Five *You shall not murder.*

Six *You shall not commit adultery.*

Seven *You shall not steal.*

Eight *You shall not bear false witness against your neighbor.*

Nine *You shall not covet your neighbor's house.*

Ten *You shall not covet your neighbor's wife, or male or female slave, or ox, or donkey, or anything that belongs to your neighbor.*

Make sure you understand the meaning of each statement. Do not hesitate to ask for clarification if something does not make sense to you. When you ask questions, you open the door to greater understanding and growth.

The Eight Beatitudes

The second passage — called the Beatitudes — is found in Matthew's Gospel (5:3–12). These statements, unlike the Ten Commandments, focus on what we must do (rather than not do) if we wish to follow the teachings of Jesus. In many ways, the Beatitudes are very challenging to the Christian because they demand that we be active!

Blessed are the poor in spirit,
for theirs is the kingdom of heaven.

Blessed are those who mourn, for they will be comforted.

Blessed are the meek, for they will inherit the earth.

Blessed are those who hunger and thirst for righteousness,
for they will be filled.

Blessed are the merciful, for they will receive mercy.

Blessed are the pure in heart, for they will see God.

Blessed are the peacemakers,
for they will be called children of God.

Blessed are those who are persecuted for righteousness' sake,
for theirs is the kingdom of heaven.

Blessed are you when people revile you and persecute you and utter all kinds of evil against you falsely on my account. Rejoice and be glad, for your reward is great in heaven, for in the same way they persecuted the prophets who were before you.

Based on the original by Michael Ketterhagen.
Special thanks to Rev. Paul Niemann and Rev. Joe Kempf.

Edited by Lauren K. Borstell. Design by Wendy Barnes.

Published with ecclesiastical approval. Compliant with *The Roman Missal*, third edition.

BILL WITTMAN

it his or her own. A candidate for confirmation, after careful review of what the Church teaches, seeks to accept these teachings as his or her own. And with acceptance must come deliberate and active involvement in the life of the faith community.

In the Eucharist, Our Spirits Are Nourished

Another name for Jesus' death and Resurrection is the "paschal mystery." Jesus is our "Lamb of God." He allowed himself to be killed, and through his suffering and death on the cross, we are able to live. In the Eucharist, this paschal mystery is celebrated. In response to Christ's gift of himself to us, we bring to God our own lives — symbolized in the bread and wine, "the work of human hands." God accepts our lives, consecrates them, and nourishes our spirits through his special presence in the Eucharist.

questions to consider

Your preparation for the sacrament of confirmation should include some real soul-searching. It is important to ask yourself the questions, "What does my baptism mean *to me?* What does it mean to have *life in the Church?*"

To help you answer these difficult questions, pretend, for a moment, that you were never baptized. Imagine that your parents and godparents never initiated you into the Christian community. Describe, in as much detail as possible, how your life would be different. (For example, what kind of moral framework might you have if you never knew Jesus? Would you have different friends? Perhaps a different school? How would you celebrate special days like Christmas and Easter if Jesus was not part of your life? Would you view death differently?) Hopefully, by imagining your life without the special sacraments of initiation, you might better be able to recognize and appreciate the many ways in which God's gift of grace influences and affects your life.

Select an adult or older sibling in your family and request that he or she grant you a short "interview." Explain that you would like to learn how this person experienced the sacraments of initiation. (If none of the members of your immediate family are Catholic, you might need to call a friend or relative whom you know has received the sacraments.) Here are a few questions that can be used for your interview — but feel free to add your own, particularly if you are interviewing someone with an unusual or interesting faith background. Again, post your interview in a very visible place for a week or two. Reflect on the unique way we are each called to holiness.

Name of person interviewed:

Date:

Relationship:

How old were you when you were baptized?

If you were old enough to remember your baptism, what, specifically, do you most remember?

When were you confirmed? Describe your preparation for this sacrament. What aspects of confirmation were most emphasized during your study and preparation?

When did you first receive the Eucharist? What do you most remember about your first experience of this sacrament?

Are you still an active participant in the life of the Church today? If so, in what ways do you serve and benefit from your faith community?

Based on the original by Michael Ketterhagen. Special thanks to Rev. Paul Niemann and Rev. Joe Kempf. Edited by Lauren K. Borstell. Design by Wendy Barnes.

The Words of Commitment

✠

To the Confirmation Candidates

Celebrant: God has called you to be God's sons and daughters in the sacrament of baptism. You have followed the Light. Now the way of the gospel opens more fully before you, inviting you to acknowledge God's love for you by asking you to commit yourself to a life of service and love, peace and justice to all. This is the way of faith on which Christ will lovingly guide you to eternal life. Are you ready to enter this journey?

Candidates: I am.

Celebrant: Are you willing to accept the Christian community as your environment for experiencing faith and growing in the Spirit?

Candidates: I am.

Celebrant: Are you willing to deepen your personal commitment to Jesus Christ and take responsibility for the gifts of the Spirit in order to help build the kingdom of God?

Candidates: I am.

To the Confirmation Sponsors

Celebrant: Are you willing to help guide these candidates for confirmation in the name of this Christian community on their journey of the Spirit?

Sponsors: I am.

To the Parish Community

Celebrant: Will you continue to renew your faith in the spirit of your own confirmation?

Community: Yes, we will.

Celebrant: Will you also support these young men and women of our Christian community as they follow Jesus and his gospel?

Community: Yes, we will.

Celebrant: Lord of love and mercy, we thank you in the name of our brothers and sisters, who have experienced your guiding presence in their lives. Today, in the presence of your community, they are promising to prepare for your coming in the sacrament of confirmation. *(The celebrant now asks the sponsors to sign the candidates to prepare them for the journey of the Spirit.)*

Receive the cross of Christ: By this sign of his love, Christ will be your strength. Learn now to know and follow him. Remember that he is your faithful companion as you study, reflect, prepare, and pray.

Candidates: Amen.

Celebrant: Lord, we pray for those just signed with the cross of our Lord Jesus Christ. By its power, keep them safe. May they be faithful to the call so that they can live with their beloved Creator in glory. We ask this through Christ our Lord.

All: Amen.

Prayer of the Faithful follows.

In this lesson, we have discussed the importance of the parish community as a source of support and strength as we strive to follow in the footsteps of our Lord Jesus. You have asked the parish family to pledge its prayers and support as you prepare to receive the sacrament of confirmation — and you have committed yourselves to study and prepare to the best of your abilities.

Now, you will seek a simple but important commitment from your own family — the promise to support you and pray for you as you seek to learn all you can about the sacrament you hope to receive in the coming months. Practically speaking, you are asking your family and loved ones to take your preparation very seriously, to assist you in finding adequate time for study and reflection, to be willing to review the lessons with you, and most importantly, to support you with their prayers.

Your families are likely the most influential members of the greater parish family in terms of your faith development, so their commitments are very helpful. Ask each member of your family (those old enough to understand) to read the following statement. If he or she is up to the challenge, he or she may sign below. Again, post this page in a place where you will see it often in the weeks ahead.

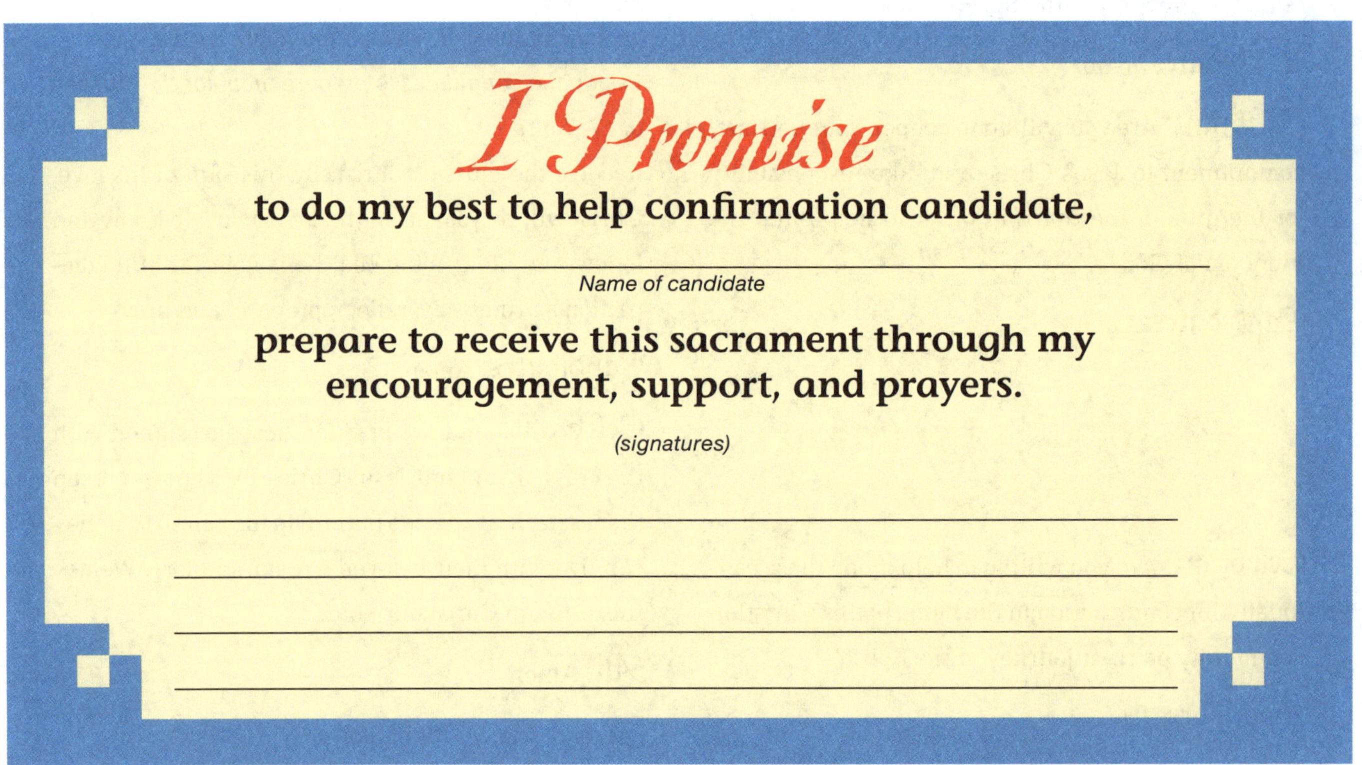

I Promise

to do my best to help confirmation candidate,

____

Name of candidate

prepare to receive this sacrament through my encouragement, support, and prayers.

(signatures)

____

____

____

____

Based on the original by Michael Ketterhagen. Special thanks to Rev. Paul Niemann and Rev. Joe Kempf. Edited by Lauren K. Borstell. Design by Wendy Barnes.

Through the sacraments, we receive *grace — a gift from God*. We do not "earn" grace through our commitments or studies. Grace is always freely given by our generous Lord who wishes to empower us through his marvelous and mysterious influence. The sacraments require *faith* because they involve "mystery."

In the weeks ahead, you will be more fully introduced to the richness of the sacrament of confirmation—a sacrament intimately linked to our baptism. Confirmation, like all sacraments, begins with a ritual, but the graces received are experienced *in every moment of our great journey.*

Questions to Consider. When we were baptized, it is likely we were too young to remember this wonderful sacrament in which we were welcomed and embraced by the Christian community. We became *children of God*. One of the objectives of adolescent confirmation is to give young men and women a sense of their own dignity and value *because of their baptisms… because they are God's precious children.* Recalling our baptisms helps us to reflect on our great value at a time when we might be doubting it.

What does it mean to be "a child of God?"

What meaning does your baptism have for you *today*?

The oil (chrism) of our baptism reminds us that we are "Priest, Prophet, and King" (from the Order of Baptism for Children). Yet, our society defines our values in many *destructive* ways. Can you give an example or two of how our modern world defines our values?

(Recall the "roads to success" discussed earlier in this lesson.)

With the help of your parents or other loved ones, recall the day of your baptism. Record a few important details.

- Date of your baptism:

....

- Your godparents:

....

- Place where you were baptized:

....

- Your age at the time of your baptism:

....

- Family members and important loved ones present to witness your baptism:

....

....

If it is possible, find a picture of yourself taken on the day of your baptism. Tape it to this paper in the space below. Hang it on your refrigerator or in some other prominent place. Over the course of the week, every time you see this paper, thank God for the gifts of life and grace received through baptism — and then remind yourself of how very much you are loved by your Creator God.

(Tape picture here.)

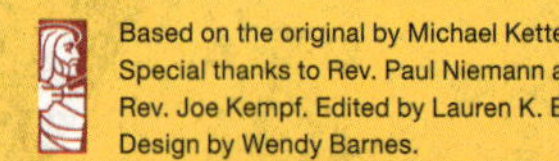

Based on the original by Michael Ketter
Special thanks to Rev. Paul Niemann ar
Rev. Joe Kempf. Edited by Lauren K. Bc
Design by Wendy Barnes.

ISBN 978-0-7648-0109-9